Wild Predators!

Deadly Snakes

Andrew Solway

www.heinemann.co.uk/library
Visit our website to find out more information about **Heinemann Library** books.

To order:
 Phone 44 (0) 1865 888066
 Send a fax to 44 (0) 1865 314091
 Visit the Heinemann Bookshop at www.heinemann.co.uk/library to browse our catalogue and order online.

First published in Great Britain by
Heinemann Library, Halley Court, Jordan Hill,
Oxford OX2 8EJ, part of Harcourt Education.
Heinemann is a registered trademark of Harcourt
Education Ltd.

© Harcourt Education Ltd 2005
First published in paperback in 2006
The moral right of the proprietor has been
asserted.

Editorial: Lucy Thunder and Harriet Milles
Design: David Poole and Paul Myerscough
Illustrations: Geoff Ward
Picture Research: Rebecca Sodergren,
Melissa Allison and Pete Morris
Production: Séverine Ribierre

Originated by Ambassador Litho Ltd.
Printed and bound in China by
South China Printing Co Ltd.
The paper used to print this book comes from
sustainable resources.

ISBN 0 431 18993 5 (hardback)
08 07 06 05 04
10 9 8 7 6 5 4 3 2 1

ISBN 0 431 18999 4 (paperback)
08 07 06 05
10 9 8 7 6 5 4 3 2 1

British Library Cataloguing in Publication Data
Solway, Andrew
Deadly Snakes. – (Wild predators)
597.9'6153
A full catalogue record for this book is available
from the British Library.

Acknowledgements
The Publishers would like to thank the following
for permission to reproduce photographs:
Animals/Joe McDonald pp**39** top, **41**;
ANTPhoto.com/Klaus Uhlenhut pp**31**, **33**;
CORBIS/Michael & Patricia Fogden pp**43** bottom,
45; CORBIS/Stephen Frink pp**32**, **34**; Digital
Vision pp**9**, **11** bottom; FLPA/Roger Wilmhurst
pp**4**, **7** bottom; Frank Lane Picture Agency/Chris
Mattison pp**2**, **5** top, **20**; Frank Lane Picture
Agency/E&D Hosking pp**26**, **27**, **36**, **38**; Frank
Lane Picture Agency/Hans Dieter Brandl pp**14**, **15**;
Frank Lane Picture Agency/L Lee Rue pp**12**, **14**;
Frank Lane Picture Agency/Mandal Ranjit p**24**;
Getty Images/Photodisc pp**15**, **16** bottom; Natural
Visions/Heather Angel p**17** bottom; Natural
Visions/Ian Took pp**33**, **35**; Nature Picture
Library/Bruce Davidson pp**10**, **8**; NHPA/Daniel
Heuclin pp**13**, **15** top, **18**, **21** top, **21**, **25** top,
25, **27** bottom, **29**, **34**, **36**, **38**, **40**, **41** top, **41**
bottom, **43** top, **44**, **47**, **48**; NHPA/ANT Photo
Library pp**30**, **32**; NHPA/Anthony Bannister pp**22**,
22, **25**, **26**, **27** top, **28**, **42**, **43**; NHPA/Gerard
Lacz pp**29**, **31**; NHPA/James Carmichael Jr pp**8**, **5**,
28, **30**; NHPA/Kevin Schafer p**19**; NHPA/Martin
Harvey pp**35**, **37**; NHPA/Martin Wendler pp**3**, **6**
bottom; Oxford Scientific Films/Avril Ramage
pp**20**, **21**; Oxford Scientific Films/Brain Kenney
pp**39** bottom, **42**; Oxford Scientific Films/David M
Dennis pp**23** top, **23**, **37**, **39**; Oxford Scientific
Films/Marty Cordano pp**10**, **12** bottom; SPL/C K
Lorenz pp**40**, **46**; SPL/Dr Morley Read pp**11**, **13**
top; SPL/Jany Sauvanet pp**6**, **9**; SPL/Jeff Lepore
pp**16**, **17** top; SPL/Renee Lynn pp**1**, **4**;
SPL/Sinclair Stammers p**7** top.

The Publishers would like to thank Rhys Jones,
Consultant Herpetologist, for his assistance in the
preparation of this book. Rhys Jones has worked
with snakes in the wild throughout the world for
over 20 years, and is an expert in handling
venomous snake species.

Contents

Any words appearing in the text in bold, **like this**, are explained in the Glossary.

Legless lizards

Snakes don't seem very promising as **predators**. Their eyesight is not very good and they have a limited range of hearing. They have a small head, a skinny body and no legs. Yet snakes are some of the most successful predators in the world.

Although snakes have no limbs (arms or legs), they can move quickly and silently on the ground, in trees and in water. They use their long, muscular, flexible bodies to hold their **prey** and stop them from struggling. Their many backward-pointing, sharp teeth are designed to stop prey escaping when they strike. And some groups of snakes have two larger teeth, or fangs, that are used to inject **venom** into the animals they eat.

Scaly reptiles

There are 3000 or so different **species** of snake, and all of them are predators. Snakes are reptiles, related to crocodiles, turtles, and most closely to lizards. Reptiles have a dry, scaly skin and are **cold-blooded**. This means that, unlike **warm-blooded** animals, they cannot keep their body at a constant temperature. They warm up or cool down depending on the temperature of their surroundings. However, snakes avoid getting too hot or too cold by behaviour such as basking in the morning sun and cooling off in water.

A spectacled cobra rising up and spreading its hood in a defensive display. The cobra's large ventral (belly) scales can be seen on its underside.

Snake, worm or lizard?

The difference
between snakes
and other animals
seems fairly obvious:
snakes don't have legs!
But a few other animals
are quite snake-like – slow
worms for instance, look very
like snakes, but are actually
lizards. So how do we tell these
apart from snakes?

Snakes have no eyelids – their eyes are
protected by a single transparent scale called
a brille (a slow worm, on the other hand, does
have eyelids). And snakes have no ear flaps
or ear openings, although they do have ears
inside their head. On its underside, a snake has
a row of large scales (the **ventral** scales) that
are not found in other animals. These act like
caterpillar tracks on a bulldozer, giving the
snake a good grip on the ground.

'Worm lizards' are not snakes,
worms or lizards, but a
separate group of animals
altogether. They differ from
snakes in that their scales are
arranged in regular rings
around their body.

Last of all, snakes have very unusual skulls. Apart from the braincase
itself, most of the bones of a snake's skull are only loosely held
together. The lower jaw can work as two separate halves, and it can
also dislocate (come apart) from the rest of the skull. This can be very
useful when swallowing large prey. Slow worms cannot dislocate their
jaw like this, nor can any other snake-like creature.

Anaconda

It is dusk in the Amazon rainforest. A **peccary** comes to drink at a still, muddy pool in the forest. As it drinks, something that looks like a small rock drifts gently across the water. Suddenly, the 'rock' rises up – it is a green anaconda. The anaconda grabs the peccary with its powerful jaws and coils itself round its victim. The peccary is doomed.

The biggest snake

The green anaconda is one of the largest snakes in the world, and definitely the heaviest. Large anacondas reach a length of 9 metres and can measure 30 centimetres around. Anacondas live in the South American rainforest. They spend most of their time in water and they usually hunt at night.

Boas and pythons

The anaconda is a boa, one of a group of large snakes found in South America. They are related to the pythons found in Africa and Asia – both groups belong to the boa **family** (family Boidae).

Boas and pythons do not have **venomous** fangs – they kill their **prey** by **constricting** (squeezing) them. The snake coils around its victim, then tightens the coils until the animal can no longer breathe or its heart stops.

The thick powerful body of an anaconda is strong enough to constrict an animal as big as a caiman (a type of alligator).

Boa constrictors are heavy-bodied like anacondas, but they are usually shorter. However, at from 3.3 to 5.5 metres long they are still giants compared to most snakes.

Night hunters

Anacondas are night hunters. They find a good hiding place and wait for prey to come along. Usually the anaconda hunts in water, because the water supports its heavy body and allows it to move easily and quickly. An anaconda's eyes and nostrils are set high on its head so that it can still see and breathe while its body is submerged. It detects its prey by feeling the ripples they make in the water as they move, and by smell. Because they are often in water, anacondas eat fish and turtles, but they also catch rats, tapirs, deer, peccaries, birds, sheep and even **caimans**.

Live birth

Most reptiles lay eggs with leathery shells, in which the young develop before hatching. In boas, and several other kinds of snake, the young develop inside the female, and she gives birth to live babies.

Pint-sized constrictors

Boas and pythons are not the only snakes that constrict their prey. Many other snakes kill big prey by constriction, not venom. Rat snakes, prairie kingsnakes and smooth snakes are all small constrictors.

Smooth snakes, like this one, are small, active hunters found in heaths and moorlands throughout Europe.

Emerald boa

The emerald boa lies curled around a branch in the darkness of the rainforest night. It picks up the faint smell of **prey** and is suddenly alert. Following the scent, the snake quietly lowers itself towards a branch where a bird is **roosting**. **Heat sensors** around the snake's mouth tell it the victim's exact position. The snake strikes, its long thin teeth piercing through the feathers to the flesh below.

Tree boas

Emerald boas are much smaller than their relatives, the anacondas. The biggest grow to about 2 metres long. They live in the trees in South American forests. Tree snakes, like the emerald boa, cannot get too big and heavy, or they would not be able to climb.

Heat sensors

Like the anaconda the emerald boa hunts at night, but it is a more active hunter. It relies mainly on its sense of smell to find its prey, but when it gets close another sense kicks in. Many of the animals that it hunts are **warm-blooded**. Like other boas and pythons, the emerald boa has pits (holes) in the skin around its mouth that can detect the heat produced by a warm body. These make it possible for the boa to strike prey accurately even in total darkness.

In this photo you can see the heat-sensing pits round the emerald boa's mouth and its cat-like eyes. Pythons and boas have eyes that are sensitive to low levels of light. The pupil is a vertical slit, as in a cat's eye.

Python twin

The green tree python, which lives in the tropical rainforests of Australia or Papua New Guinea, is an almost exact twin of the emerald boa. It is about the same size, the same brilliant green colour and it hunts similar prey among the trees. Like the emerald boa, it also has heat sensors around its mouth.

However, there are some important differences between the two **species**. The most important difference is that the emerald boa produces live young, like the anaconda, but the green tree python is like other pythons and lays eggs.

Adaptation

These two snakes are excellent examples of the way in which two species that are not closely related but live in similar environments can come to look very similar. Both the boa and the python have **adapted** in similar ways to living in rainforests. These adaptations have led to them looking much more like each other than like their closer relatives.

In both the emerald boa and the green tree python, young snakes are bright yellow or dusky red rather than green. Scientists are not sure why they are a different colour when young. This photo shows a young emerald boa.

African rock python

The grasslands are parched and yellow, but storm clouds cover the sky. The dry season is at an end. As the first rains fall, a snake emerges from a hollow log. Its thick, muscular body is over 6 metres long. This African python has been **dormant** through the dry season. Now it is hungry, and ready to attack almost anything.

Big game hunters

African or rock pythons are the biggest snakes in Africa. They grow up to 8.5 metres long, although they are more usually 5.5 to 6 metres in length. They are found in grasslands and near water throughout central and southern Africa.

Like anacondas, African pythons hunt at night, and often ambush their **prey** in water. They are fierce hunters and can catch monkeys, pigs, jackals and antelopes. Large African pythons have attacked people.

Swallowing prey whole

African pythons are **constrictors**, like other members of the boa **family**. They have long teeth and a strong bite, but like other snakes, they cannot tear up their prey. Instead they swallow them whole. The snake's stomach has extra-strong **acids** to digest the prey quickly.

An African python eating a rat. Snakes nearly always eat large prey head-first. A big animal can take several weeks to digest. During this time the snake is heavy and sluggish, so it hides away.

It's hard to imagine how a snake, even a large python, could swallow an antelope whole. But a snake's jawbones are connected by stretchy **ligaments**, and it can dislocate (disconnect) its lower jaw from the rest of the skull. This allows it to open its mouth very wide indeed. The two halves of the lower jaw can also move apart, to allow the snake to swallow prey wider than its head.

Egg-sitting

Like other pythons, female African pythons lay eggs, rather than giving birth to live young. A really large female can lay 100 eggs at one time. Most snakes have nothing more to do with their eggs once they have laid them, but female pythons coil themselves around their eggs until the young hatch out. An African python's eggs take 2 or 3 months to hatch. The young can look after themselves as soon as they are born. They eat food such as mice, young **mammals** and birds.

The world's longest snake

Although the anaconda and the African python are both heavier, the longest python in the world is the reticulated python. The biggest one officially confirmed is just over 10 metres long. However, owners of a zoo in Indonesia have reported one of 14.85 metres long! Reticulated pythons, like this one, ambush their prey by dropping on them from trees. They eat mainly small mammals and birds, but can kill animals as big as deer.

Texas thread snake

The tiny, pinkish brown snake moves along an underground tunnel crowded with soldier termites. The termites have fearsome looking jaws, but they take no notice of the snake. At the end of the tunnel is a chamber filled with white termite **larvae**. The snake begins to eat them, one by one.

Tiny burrowers

Thread snakes (or slender blind snakes) are at the opposite end of the scale from boas and pythons. Thread snakes (**family** Leptotyphlopidae) and their close relatives the blind snakes (family Typhlopidae) are all small – none grow longer than 50 centimetres, and some are much smaller.

Texas thread snakes live in southwestern USA and northern Mexico, often in desert areas. Like most thread snakes and blind snakes, they eat ants and termites. Often they prefer eggs and larvae rather than adults, as these are soft and easier to eat.

Smell trails

Texas thread snakes find their food by smell. Wherever they go, ants and termites leave trails of special chemicals that other members of the nest can follow. Thread snakes can also follow these chemical trails to find ant and termite nests.

Thread snakes have small eyes – they spend most of their lives underground, where eyes are of little use.

Immune to attack

Few small animals feed on ants and termites because they have such formidable defences. These insects have a nasty bite and can spray a stinging **acid** at an attacker. If one ant or termite is attacked, it releases a chemical alarm signal that soon brings hundreds of others to help.

Thread snakes have found ingenious ways of avoiding being attacked by ants and termites. One way they do this is by producing another kind of chemical smell, which calms down the fierce soldier ants or termites that guard the nest.

Blind snakes are close relatives of thread snakes. The dwarf blind snake is perhaps the smallest snake of all. Adults are only 10 centimetres long.

Not too cold

Because they live underground, Texas thread snakes avoid the worst of the desert heat. Burrowing snakes can cool down in hot weather by going deeper into the ground, but it is difficult for them to warm up if the weather gets cold. For this reason, thread snakes and other burrowers are found only in warmer parts of the world.

Primitive snakes

Thread snakes and blind snakes are 'primitive': this means that they are most like the **ancestors** from which all snakes are descended. The earliest ancestors of snakes were lizard-like animals. Over time, they gradually lost their legs, shoulders and **pelvis**. Thread snakes are unusual because they still have some small bones that are the remains of the pelvis and hind (back) legs, although boas and pythons also have these bones.

Racer snakes

A boy is wandering along a grassy trail in North America when he hears a rattling sound. It sounds like a rattlesnake! He looks carefully around and spots a slim, black snake. It's not a rattler after all – but what is it?

Speedy snakes

When threatened, racer snakes vibrate their tails on dry leaves, imitating the sound of a rattlesnake. Racers and whip snakes are members of the colubrid **family** of snakes (Colubridae), the largest of the snake families. Over 70 per cent of all snakes are colubrids.

As their name suggests, racers are slim, fast-moving snakes. They live in many parts of North America. Racers in different areas can be different colours and have various names (for example, black racer, yellow-bellied racer), but they are all very closely related. They can grow to almost 2 metres in length, and are among the longest snakes in North America. They lay eggs rather than giving birth to live young.

Hunting by day

Racers hunt in daylight, so they have large eyes, with round pupils rather than the vertical slits of night-hunters. But a racer snake's eyesight is not as good as that of a **mammal** or bird **predator**. Racers use their excellent sense of smell to follow the scent trails of their **prey**.

The black racer is normally a glossy black colour, although young snakes are patterned in black and grey. For snakes, they move very fast: they can reach speeds of 10 km/h (7 mph) for short distances.

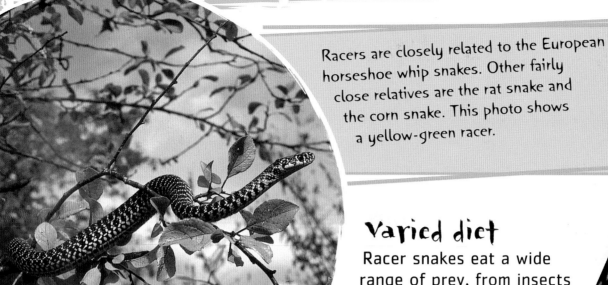

Racers are closely related to the European horseshoe whip snakes. Other fairly close relatives are the rat snake and the corn snake. This photo shows a yellow-green racer.

Varied diet

Racer snakes eat a wide range of prey, from insects to rats and other small mammals. They will also eat other snakes. Racers do not have **venomous** fangs, but they do not **constrict** their prey either. Instead they use a loop of their body to hold their prey down and bite it repeatedly.

Smelling in stereo

Snakes have smell sensors in their nose and they also pick up smells using their tongue and mouth. When snakes flick their tongue in and out of their mouth, they pick up smell chemicals from the air. These chemicals are passed on to a smell sensor on the roof of the mouth, called the Jacobson's organ.

Because the end of a snake's tongue is forked, the two tips taste different amounts of chemicals. This means a snake 'smells in stereo' and can work out which direction a smell is coming from.

A horseshoe whip snake testing the air with its forked tongue.

15

Garter snakes

The garter snake has been basking in the late afternoon sun, but now it is ready to hunt. It glides along the riverbank, head held up, tasting the air as it goes. As it approaches a clump of reeds, a frog jumps into the water with a plop. The garter snake follows, as comfortable hunting in water as on land.

Active hunters

Garter snakes are common snakes in most of North America. Like racers they belong to the colubrid **family**. There are several kinds of garter snake. The biggest can grow to 160 centimetres, but commonly they are about 60 to 80 centimetres long. Garter snakes hunt a wide range of **prey**, including worms and insects, fish, frogs, newts and mice.

Garter snakes are active hunters. They follow promising scent trails, and poke around in places where prey might hide. They also hunt in water, swimming along with their mouth open. Like racers, garter snakes bite and hold their prey, rather than **constricting** them. They are not **venomous**, but scientists think that chemicals in their saliva may help them to overcome prey.

Garter snakes get their name from the striped patterns on their body. The patterns are similar to those on old-fashioned garters that men used to wear to hold up their socks.

Beating the cold

Garter snakes are found further north than any other American snakes. They survive the cold by **hibernating** through the winter, but they can stay active until late in the autumn. Garter snakes can even survive brief periods of being frozen! They hibernate in sheltered places such as burrows or hollow logs. They usually gather in small groups, but at good hibernating sites there may be thousands of snakes.

When spring comes, males come out of hibernation first to warm up in the sunshine. When the females emerge, groups of males rush to **mate** with each female. Eventually one male will mate with the female, and 2 or 3 months later the female gives birth to between 3 and 50 live young.

In spring, hundreds of male garter snakes form a writhing mass, fighting to mate with one female.

European cousins

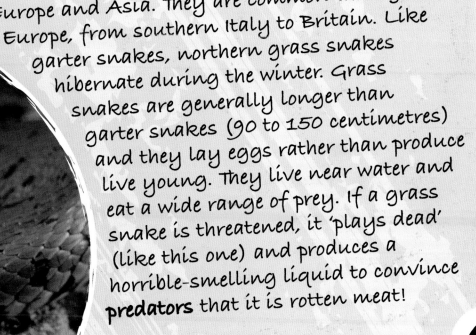

Grass snakes are relatives of garter snakes that are found in Europe and Asia. They are common throughout Europe, from southern Italy to Britain. Like garter snakes, northern grass snakes hibernate during the winter. Grass snakes are generally longer than garter snakes (90 to 150 centimetres) and they lay eggs rather than produce live young. They live near water and eat a wide range of prey. If a grass snake is threatened, it 'plays dead' (like this one) and produces a horrible-smelling liquid to convince **predators** that it is rotten meat!

Asian vine snake

A lizard runs along a leafy branch in the Malaysian forest, then stops briefly. Close to where it stops, a twig sways in the breeze. The lizard doesn't notice the twig – but the twig notices the lizard! With a snap it catches the lizard by the throat and begins to choke it. The 'twig' is actually an Asian vine snake.

Hawkeye hunters

Asian vine snakes (also known as long-nosed tree snakes) are found in the tropical forests of India, Sri Lanka and South-east Asia. They are slim (a bit thicker than a finger), medium-sized snakes, 60 to 200 centimetres long. Like garter snakes and racers, they are daytime hunters.

The long nose and unusual eyes of the Asian vine snake give it sharp vision and help it to judge distances accurately.

More than any other snake, the Asian vine snake relies on its eyesight for hunting. Its eyes and head are well-**adapted** for this purpose. Vine snakes have large eyes with an unusually shaped pupil – like a figure 8 on its side. This kind of pupil helps the snake to judge distances accurately. The vine snake also has a long, unusually shaped nose, with grooves on either side of it, in front of the eyes. These grooves give the snake a clear view directly ahead, so that it can focus more clearly on its **prey**.

The lizards and tree frogs that the vine snake eats are often well **camouflaged**. When a snake comes along they freeze, which makes them even harder to see. Most snakes cannot see prey that is still, but the vine snake, with its excellent eyesight, can pick out motionless lizards and frogs from their background.

'Chewing' fangs

Some snakes in the colubrid **family** have **venomous** fangs. They are known as rear-fanged snakes, because their fangs are at the back of the mouth. The Asian vine snake is a rear-fanged snake. Like most other rear-fanged snakes, it is harmless to humans, but its venom is **fatal** to the lizards and tree frogs that it hunts.

At the front of its mouth the vine snake has a set of sharp, backward-pointing teeth. It uses these to bite prey when it first strikes. Asian vine snakes often choke their victims with this first strike. The vine snake's fangs are behind these front teeth. They are grooved, and get their venom from **glands** just below the eye. If a lizard or frog is not killed quickly, the vine snake shifts it to the back of the mouth and begins to chew. Chewing injects venom deep into the prey's body.

The Asian vine snake 'chews' on large prey, like this frog, to inject the venom from its rear fangs.

19

Paradise flying snake

A smallish, dark snake with red bands across its back slithers along the branch of a tree in Burma. It reaches the end of the branch and hangs from its tail, with the head lifted so that the body forms a J-shape. Then with a flick, the snake launches itself into the air.

An S-shaped wing

The paradise flying snake is about 1 metre long. It lives in the Asian rainforest and feeds mainly on lizards. Like the vine snake it has rear fangs and it is not dangerous to humans. What makes the paradise flying snake extraordinary is its ability to fly. In fact, paradise flying snakes are actually gliders, rather than fliers – they can glide downwards but cannot fly up.

The long, thin body of a snake does not seem like a very good shape for gliding, but paradise flying snakes have a few tricks up their sleeve. When a paradise snake throws itself from a branch, it 'sucks in its stomach' and spreads its ribs out sideways. This makes the snake wider, and its underside is curved upwards. The whole body becomes like a long, thin parachute.

In studies of the gliding ability of paradise tree snakes, scientists found that for every metre a snake fell vertically, it could travel nearly 4 metres horizontally.

Lizard hunters

Paradise flying snakes are tree-dwellers like vine snakes. Their round pupils show that they are daytime hunters. They hunt small **prey** such as lizards, frogs, birds and bats.

This paradise flying snake is eating a rat. It is one of five known kinds of flying snake. All of them live in the forests of South Asia.

They stalk or chase prey animals and bite them on the neck. Paradise flying snakes are such good gliders that they could attack prey by dropping on them from above. However, this kind of hunting has not been observed.

Skinned alive

The grass snake on the left is shedding its skin. A snake's scales are not separate, like those on a fish. They are thickened areas of the snake's skin, which cover its whole body. A snake's skin does not grow with its body, as human skin does. Instead, snakes shed their skin as they grow – usually several times per year.

Just before a snake sheds its skin, its colours go dull and its eyes become cloudy. Shedding begins from the head. Tree-living **species** often help the shedding process along by hooking the old skin over a branch and pulling away from it. Shedding its skin makes a snake vulnerable to attack, so before doing it, a snake hides away and does not hunt.

Boomslang

The scientist puts on his gloves, and picks up the boomslang. Then he takes a pad of foam and presses it gently against the snake's mouth. The boomslang bites, injecting a tiny amount of **venom** into the foam. Venom from many such 'snake milkings' will be used to make **antivenom**, for treating people with snake bites.

Looking like a twig

Boomslangs are rear-fanged colubrid snakes that live in **savannah** and open woodland areas in Africa. The biggest boomslangs are almost 2 metres long.

Boomslangs spend most of their time in trees. Their large eyes and round pupils show that they are daytime hunters. A boomslang often hunts by wrapping most of its body around a tree branch, leaving just the front part sticking up like a twig. It stays motionless in this position, waiting for a lizard or other small animal to come by. Like vine snakes, boomslangs usually strike first with their front teeth, then move the victim further into the mouth and 'chew' on it to inject venom.

Different colours

Male boomslangs can have a variety of colours and patterns, while females are a uniform brown colour. Female boomslangs lay eggs rather than producing live young. When the young hatch, they are differently coloured from both adult males and females – dark above and lighter coloured below.

Male, female and young boomslangs have different colouration and markings. This is unusual in snakes, probably because most kinds of snake do not have good enough eyesight to be able to see such differences. This photo is of a female boomslang.

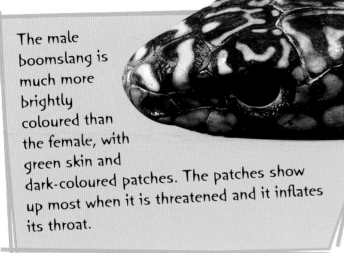

The male boomslang is much more brightly coloured than the female, with green skin and dark-coloured patches. The patches show up most when it is threatened and it inflates its throat.

Deadly fangs

Most rear-fanged snakes are not dangerous to humans, but boomslangs have very toxic (poisonous) venom. A few drops are enough to kill a human. A few people have died from boomslang bites, but this is quite uncommon. Boomslangs are much more likely to retreat from people than to strike. Also, their fangs are short and can deliver only small amounts of venom. More importantly, the fangs are at the back of the snake's mouth, so it needs a long 'chew' to inject venom rather than making a quick strike.

Deadly or dangerous?

Snakes with deadly venom are not necessarily dangerous to people. Coral snakes, for instance, have deadly venom, but their mouth and fangs are small, so it is hard for them to give a serious bite. Also they live underground, where humans rarely come across them.

Other snakes with less deadly venom can cause more deaths. Puff adders, for instance, have large fangs and produce lots of venom. They often lie still so they are almost invisible on forest tracks, and it is easy for people to step on them and get bitten.

King cobra

A man is walking his dog by a river in Malaysia. The dog trots off to investigate a thicket of bamboo near the water. As it sniffs around, a low, growling hiss comes from inside the thicket. The dog yelps and runs back to its owner. It has disturbed a female king cobra on her nest.

Snake-hunters

King cobras are the largest **venomous** snakes in the world. The biggest are over 5 metres in length. They are part of a **family** of snakes called the elapids (Elapidae). All elapids are venomous and have small, fixed fangs in the front of their mouth.

King cobras are found across southern and eastern Asia. They live in warm, wet places with dense undergrowth, such as rainforests and swamps. King cobras specialize in hunting snakes, sometimes deadly snakes such as kraits. They will even eat other king cobras.

A king cobra has 2 small, hollow fangs at the front of its mouth. When it attacks, it lifts up the front part of its body and strikes down with these fangs. The king cobra's venom is dangerous to humans and the cobra can inject large amounts of it – enough to kill an elephant!

Although they are large and dangerous, king cobras rarely attack people. If threatened, they make themselves look more dangerous by rearing up and spreading their necks into a 'hood'.

Nest-builders

King cobras **mate** between January and March, and about 3 months later the female lays her eggs on a pile of leaves and twigs she has prepared. She coils up on top of the pile to keep guard. King cobras are the only snakes that build nests.

King cobras have only a narrow hood compared to most other cobras.

A female king cobra on her nest.

The female guards the eggs for about 2 months, during which time she does not eat. Just before the eggs hatch, she leaves the nest. Scientists think this is because, after 2 months without food, females that stayed with their offspring would not be able to resist eating them when they hatched.

Disappearing habitat

King cobras are not a threatened **species** but, as for so many other animals, their **habitat** is being reduced by human activities. One of the main threats to cobra habitat is shrimp farming, because many **mangrove** swamps have been cut down and replaced with shrimp farms. Sea snakes, pythons and other snake species also live in mangrove swamps and are affected by their destruction.

There are about 20 other kinds of cobra besides the king cobra. Spitting cobras bite their **prey** as do other snakes, but if they are threatened they spit venom in the eyes of their enemy.

Black mamba

The wilderness guide stops and holds up his hand. 'Stay very still', he orders. In front of the tour group, a large, dark snake is coiled round a bush. The snake stares at the people and everyone holds their breath. Then in a flash of speed it is gone, leaving only a ripple in the grass. 'A black mamba!' breathes the guide.

Speedy snakes

Black mambas are fast-moving, **venomous** snakes that live in **savannah** and open woodland in Africa. Most mambas are around 3 metres or so, but the biggest can be up to 4.5 metres long, making it the world's second-longest venomous snake.

Black mambas are also the fastest snakes in the world: reaching speeds of up to 23 km/hr (14 mph). This is no faster than a fit adult can run, but over rough ground and through undergrowth it can move far faster than a human.

Like cobras, black mambas are elapids – they have small, fixed fangs. However, a black mamba's venom is very different from a king cobra's. It is powerful and very fast acting and the mamba can deliver large amounts in a single bite. A mamba bite can kill a human in as little as 15 minutes.

Matchless hunters

At night, black mambas rest in a permanent den: often a termite mound or an animal burrow. In the morning the mamba usually finds a rock to bask on, to raise its body temperature after the cool of the night. Then it goes hunting.

This black mamba is being 'milked' for its venom. Black mambas are not black, but grey or brownish. They get their name from the black lining of the mouth.

Despite their length, black mambas are agile climbers. They often climb trees and bushes in search of nesting birds or other prey.

When hunting, black mambas move rapidly, with up to a third of their body lifted off the ground. They eat birds, mice, rats, and other small **mammals**. Mambas have excellent eyesight, a superb sense of smell and can sense the vibrations of moving animals through the ground. Their speed, sharp senses and powerful venom make them matchless **predators**.

Mambas and people

People fear black mambas – if there is a mamba around, most people will want it killed. It is true that mambas are very dangerous snakes, but in fact they often live successfully quite close to humans. Rivers, canals and irrigation ditches make excellent routes for mambas to find their way to and from farm buildings and gardens, where they catch mice, birds and other **prey**. Mambas have even been found warming themselves on car engines or looped around toilets. Mambas tolerate people, but we aren't very good at tolerating them!

Green mambas are smaller, less aggressive, relatives of the black mamba. They live almost entirely in the trees.

Coral snake

A girl is raking leaves in Arizona, USA. She suddenly catches sight of a flash of colour among the leaves: bright red and yellow. Moving the leaves aside with the rake, she uncovers a tiny jewel of a snake, no thicker than her finger. The snake looks so attractive she wants to pick it up. But luckily she knows about coral snakes, so she keeps her distance.

Tiny jewels

Coral snakes are brilliantly-coloured snakes with a wicked bite. There are about 65 kinds of coral snake worldwide. They live in hot, tropical regions of North and South America, South-east Asia and Australia.

Coral snakes are fairly small – some are only 30 centimetres long – and the thickness of a pencil. They belong to the elapid **family**, and like other elapids they are highly **venomous**.

Over 50 different kinds of coral snake are found in the Americas, from Argentina in South America to Texas in the USA. This is an Eastern coral snake.

Underground hunters

Coral snakes are night hunters, and their main **prey** are other burrowing snakes. They spend most of their time underground or hidden under rocks. However, some Asian coral snakes live in water and hunt eels.

Coral snakes have small mouths and their fangs are tiny. However, their venom is powerful and quickly kills its prey. A bite from a coral snake can kill a human, but because they live mostly underground they have caused very few human deaths.

Reproducing

Coral snakes lay eggs rather than producing live young. The female lays her eggs about 40 days after **mating**, and the eggs hatch 2 to 3 months later. The young are born with fully developed fangs and venom, and are able to hunt almost as soon as they hatch.

Colourful warning

Coral snakes have few **predators** because their poison is deadly to most animals. The snake's bright colours warn other predators that they are poisonous. However, if a coral snake is threatened, it sometimes hides its head and lifts its tail, curling the tip over to look like a head. It also produces a horrible-smelling liquid and spreads it all over its attacker.

Copycat corals

In areas where coral snakes live, there are often other, non-venomous snakes with similar warning colours. These copycats, or mimics, have similar colours to avoid being eaten by predators.

In the USA, milk snakes and kingsnakes, like this one, mimic coral snakes – but their red and yellow bands of colour are separated from each other, whereas in coral snakes the red and yellow bands touch. Predators learn that snakes with bright bands are dangerous, so they avoid eating the mimics as well as the real thing.

Taipan

The rat hears the snake coming, and scuttles away across the rubbish tip. But the taipan catches up with the rat and strikes. Its long fangs sink through the rat's fur and into its body. The taipan does not hang on to the rat but pulls away and strikes again, and then a third time. Soon the **venom** takes effect and the rat is dead.

Where to find taipans

Taipans live in Australia and Papua New Guinea. There are two kinds. The common taipan is a giant snake, about as long as a black mamba (around 3.3 metres). It is found in many parts of northern Australia and Papua New Guinea. The inland taipan is smaller and lives in dry desert areas.

Taipans are elapids, and over half the snakes in Australia belong to the elapid **family**. It is the only part of the world where venomous snakes outnumber non-venomous ones.

Taipans are large, aggressive snakes with deadly venom and large fangs which they bare when attacking prey.

Rat-catchers

Taipans are active, daytime hunters. Inland taipans hunt in the morning and evening, when the desert is cooler. Taipans most often hunt rats and mice, although common taipans also catch larger **prey**. With small prey such as mice a taipan will strike and hold on, but with larger prey it strikes, releases, then strikes again. This way it avoids being injured by the struggles of its victim.

These snakes produce large amounts of venom. One good bite from a taipan contains enough venom to kill 50,000 mice!

Taipans and humans

Humans rarely come across inland taipans, but the common taipan has **adapted** to living around humans. It often hunts in sugar-cane fields and on rubbish tips, where rats and mice are common. Taipans are large, fast and aggressive snakes – and drop for drop, their venom is more powerful than that of any other land snake. If they are threatened they will attack and strike repeatedly. An angry taipan is probably one of the most dangerous snakes in the world.

Snake antivenoms

Until **antivenoms** were developed in 1955, almost every person bitten by a taipan died from the bite. Since that time, antivenoms have saved many lives.

Antivenoms are the only way to treat the bites of many venomous snakes. They are made by 'milking' snakes of their venom (see page 26), then injecting tiny quantities of this venom into horses or sheep. The animals make **antibodies** to the venom in their blood. An extract of the animal's blood is then used as antivenom. Different snake bites need different antivenoms, so unless they are absolutely certain which snake has bitten a victim, doctors use an antivenom mixture.

Sea snakes

Floating tail-first on the ocean surface, like a kind of living seaweed, is a group of yellow-bellied sea snakes. A shoal of fish takes shelter under the 'seaweed', thinking it a good place to hide from **predators**. As an unwary fish swims closer to the surface, one snake strikes downwards with a snap of its jaws. The fish hardly struggles – the snake's **venom** is so powerful that its victim dies almost immediately.

The commonest snakes

Sea snakes are a sub-**family** of the elapids that live entirely in the sea. They are found in warm waters around the world. Most sea snakes live in shallow waters, but a few, like the yellow-bellied sea snake, travel the open ocean. Scientists estimate that there are more sea snakes than land snakes.

Well adapted

Sea snakes are well **adapted** to their watery life. Their bodies are flattened towards the back into a vertical paddle-shaped tail, which they move up and down to power them through the water. They have an elongated lung, which allows them to take in extra air so they can stay underwater for an hour or more. Some kinds also absorb **oxygen** from the water through their skin.

A sea snake swimming. The photo shows how the snake's body, and especially the tail, is flattened to help it swim.

Sea snakes shed their skin more often than land snakes, probably to get rid of barnacles and other **parasites**. Snakes in shallow water rub themselves against the seabed to shed, but snakes in deep water twist and contort themselves to get rid of their old skins.

One group of sea snakes, the sea kraits, comes ashore to lay their eggs. But other sea snakes never leave the sea: they give birth to live young in the water.

Hunting in the water

Sea snakes hunt various kinds of fish. The olive sea snake corners fish in a crevice. It then injects them with a paralysing poison from its fangs and swallows the **prey** whole. Another **species**, the beaked sea snake, catches catfish or puffer fish and feeds on dead fish caught in fishing nets. Like other sea snakes, the beaked sea snake has extremely poisonous venom. Its venom is even more deadly than the taipan's.

Deadly venom reduces the chances of the prey escaping or injuring the sea snake. However, sea snakes are rarely dangerous to humans. They have small fangs, they live in areas where people are unlikely to meet them, and they will swim away rather than bite.

Puffer fish are highly poisonous, but this doesn't seem to stop sea snakes eating them. Puffer fish get their name from their habit of swelling up to twice their normal size when they are threatened.

Gaboon viper

On the floor of the African rainforest, a large, heavy-bodied snake lies among the leaves in a pool of dappled sunlight. It has just eaten a small deer and is ready to rest. The snake yawns, to get its jaws back into place after swallowing its **prey**. Lying along the top of its mouth, each in its own sheath of skin, are two enormous fangs.

Hinged-fang snakes

Gaboon vipers are thick-bodied, heavy snakes that live in African rainforests. They are the largest vipers in Africa, growing to a length of over 2 metres and a weight of 20 kilograms. They belong to the viper **family** of snakes (Viperidae). Like the elapids, vipers have **venomous** fangs at the front of their mouth. However, viper fangs are much bigger than those of elapids. Elapids have small fangs because if they were any larger the snakes would bite themselves when they shut their mouths. Vipers get round this problem by having fangs that are hinged at the base. When they are not in use, the fangs fold back against the roof of the mouth.

Gaboon vipers have the longest fangs of any snake. They can grow to 5.5 centimetres long. When the fangs are not being used, they are covered over by a flap of skin, as you can see in this picture.

Sit-and-wait predators

Gaboon vipers kept in zoos are very sluggish. They never seem to do anything. But in their forest homes they don't do very much either! Gaboon vipers don't chase after their prey – they wait for their victims to come to them. In the patchy light of the forest floor, the gaboon viper's markings provide amazingly good **camouflage**, and the snake is almost invisible unless it moves.

When a suitable prey animal comes along (any **mammal** up to the size of a small antelope), the viper raises its head and strikes. The strike is as heavy as a boxer's punch. As the viper strikes, it opens its mouth wide and swings its huge fangs into place, stabbing deep into the victim.

Gaboon viper venom is not particularly powerful, but the snake has large amounts of venom in huge venom **glands** on either side of its skull. It also has very large muscles at the back of the head that help to inject the venom quickly. These muscles and the large venom glands give vipers their characteristic triangular-shaped head.

Against a plain background, gaboon vipers have striking markings. But among the fallen leaves on the forest floor, the markings provide superb camouflage.

Live babies

Like nearly all other vipers, female gaboon vipers give birth to live young. They rarely produce more than 15 or 20 young, but the gaboon viper's close relative, the puff adder, may give birth to over 100 young at one time.

Adder

Spring is arriving on the bleak Russian **tundra**. A watery sun is shining, but it is still cold. Among the patches of melting snow an adder lies sunning itself. It has spent the winter sleeping and today is its first time above ground for 8 months.

Tough customers

Adders are part of the viper **family**. They are **venomous**, but their venom is not particularly dangerous to humans. Adders are sit-and-wait **predators**. Their black and brown patterning provides excellent **camouflage**, breaking up the snake's outline. **Prey** animals, such as voles, mice and lizards, often do not see the adder as it lies in wait. When they come close, it attacks with a lightning strike.

No other snake can survive the cold as well as the adder. It lives in a wider range of places than any other snake – from the tundra of northern Scandinavia and Russia to the warm shores of the Mediterranean.

Adapting to conditions

To survive in such a range of different conditions, the adder has to be **adaptable**. Across most of its range it is a daytime hunter, but in warmer areas it is active mornings and evenings, avoiding the heat of the day. In colder areas, adders **hibernate** for 8 months of the year. In warmer areas, they remain active all year.

This photo shows a female adder with her young. Wherever they live, adders look remarkably similar – smallish snakes up to a maximum of 80 centimetres long, with a dark zigzag pattern along the back and a dark 'V' on the head.

Reproduction

Adders **mate** in the spring, and females give birth to around 6 to 10 live young 3 or 4 months later. It takes a lot of energy for a female to produce young. In northern areas there may not be time for females who have given birth to get back to full weight and health before the winter. So in these areas females often **reproduce** once every 2 years rather than every year.

Dangerous relations

Adders are not dangerous to humans, although their bite can be very painful. Other vipers are a different matter. The puff adder causes more human deaths in Africa than any other snake, while Russell's viper causes the most deaths in southern Asia.

The deadly saw-scaled viper in this photograph is small (usually about 60 centimetres), which makes it hard to spot. It is probably the most dangerous snake in the world and causes many deaths each year in Africa, India and the Middle East. It gets its name from its rough scales, which it rubs together to make a rasping noise when threatened.

Cottonmouth

A young cottonmouth snake lies curled up among vegetation at the edge of a marshy pool. Its brown and black body is hard to see, but its bright yellow tail stands out. The young cottonmouth wriggles this tail tip temptingly – it looks like a yellow worm. A passing frog tries to snap up the 'worm', but it gets snapped up itself by the cottonmouth.

Pit vipers

Cottonmouths are vipers, but they belong to a group of snakes within the viper **family** known as the pit vipers. Pit vipers have **heat sensors** on their head, like the pythons and boas. In pit vipers, the sensors are in two 'pits' (holes), one on either side of the face between the eye and the nostril. A viper's pits are more sensitive than the heat sensors of pythons and boas (see page 8).

Cottonmouths are thick-bodied snakes between 120 and 150 centimetres long. They live in or near water in south-eastern USA. Adult cottonmouths are mainly dark above and lighter below, but young cottonmouths have strong markings and a bright yellow tail.

Cottonmouths hunt at night in or near water. During the day they often bask in the sun, warming up after the night's hunting.

Night hunters

The cottonmouth is a night hunter. It eats almost any **prey** it can find that is the right size – fish, frogs, lizards, small turtles, other water snakes, baby alligators, birds and small **mammals**. When hunting, the cottonmouth finds a good place to hide and lies in wait for prey.

A young cottonmouth uses its yellow tail tip as a lure for prey.

Cottonmouths sense prey either by smell or by feeling the vibrations of its movements. If the prey is **warm-blooded**, the cottonmouth's heat sensors help it to strike accurately.

Once it has struck, the cottonmouth keeps its jaws clamped tight round its victim, rather than letting go and waiting for the **venom** to work. This is probably because it catches most of its prey in water, and it would not be able to follow the prey's scent trail in water if it escaped.

Threat display

Cottonmouths tend to live and hunt in one area, or **territory**. If a cottonmouth is approached by a human within its territory, it will often stand its ground. When threatened, the cottonmouth coils itself up and opens its mouth wide to show the white, cottony lining. This threat display is what gives the snake its name.

A bite from a cottonmouth can cause a person serious harm, and may occasionally be **fatal**. However, very few people have actually been killed by cottonmouth snake bites.

The cottonmouth gets its name from the white, cottony-looking lining of its mouth.

Western diamondback rattlesnake

In a forest in California, USA, a man comes out of his cabin to get wood for a fire. As he picks up the first log, he hears a long, low rattle. He drops the log and steps slowly back – there is a rattlesnake on the woodpile. The rattler stares at the man, its tail still shaking noisily. Then it slides down from the wood and disappears into the undergrowth.

A noisy warning

The western diamondback is one of the biggest and most dangerous of the rattlesnakes. In North America, western diamondbacks, and their cousins the eastern diamondbacks, can cause human deaths from snake bites, although they actually kill very few people. Western diamondbacks live in the south-western USA in **habitats** that range from deserts to lush forests. They also find their way into fields, backyards and woodpiles.

Rattlesnakes get their name from the rattle on their tail, which they shake as a warning if threatened. All rattlesnakes are pit vipers, with **heat sensors** in pits on their face. The western diamondback is a night-hunter, that feeds on mice, rats, ground squirrels and rabbits. It may lie in ambush by animal trails, or attack victims in their burrows.

Western diamondbacks are usually about 1 to 1.5 metres long. Their relatives, the eastern diamondbacks, can be larger, but they are less likely to bite if disturbed.

A rattlesnake's rattle gets one section longer each time the snake sheds its skin. However, after a time the oldest rattles often break off.

The rattlesnake year

Western diamondbacks are usually active from spring to autumn, then **hibernate** in winter. Large groups hibernate together in rocky caves or crevices. In spring, males look for females to **mate** with. They often have wrestling contests over a female, twining around each other and trying to force their opponent to the ground.

In late summer females give birth to 9 or 10 live young. The young diamondbacks are about 25 centimetres long, and fully equipped with poison fangs and **venom**.

Many enemies

Young western diamondbacks have many enemies. They may become a meal for an eagle or hawk, a roadrunner, a kingsnake, a coyote or a fox. Even deer and sheep are a threat because they can accidentally trample young rattlesnakes to death.

Rattlesnakes in danger

Although no rattlesnakes are officially **endangered**, numbers in some **species**, such as the eastern diamondback and the timber rattlesnake, are falling rapidly. The main reasons are that their habitats are being destroyed, and that they are killed for food, or as pests, or to sell as pets.

Sidewinder

The moon shines on a white sand dune in Death Valley, USA. The moonlight shows up a series of strange, J-shaped marks on the dune. The marks continue over the dune and into the ruins of an old mining town. Half-buried in the sand under an ancient mining wagon, a sidewinder lies coiled and alert for **prey**.

Desert rattlers

Sidewinders are rattlesnakes that live in desert regions in North America. They are quite small rattlesnakes, growing to a maximum length of about 80 centimetres. Like other vipers they are **venomous**, and they are not afraid to attack. Their bite is extremely painful, but rarely kills humans.

Adapted for life on sand

The sidewinder gets its name from the unusual way that it moves over shifting sand. It moves in a diagonal looping movement, with only two small areas of the body touching the ground at any one time. The movement leaves a set of characteristic J-shaped marks on the ground. Sidewinding is a very efficient way of moving over shifting sand or loose soil. Several other snakes that live in deserts also use sidewinding to get about.

The sidewinder has other **adaptations** to desert life. It is sandy in colour, and its rough scales have the texture of sand. In its natural **habitat** this colouration gives it excellent **camouflage**.

A sidewinder's looping motion is the best way to get around on loose, shifting ground.

The horns over a sidewinder's eyes fold over the eye like eyelids if they are pressed down. This probably helps protect its eyes when burrowing.

Sidewinders often avoid the worst of the desert heat by burying their bodies in the sand, leaving only their eyes and nostrils showing. Over each eye the sidewinder has a small 'horn'. A similar horn is found in other desert vipers, such as the horned viper of South Africa. The horns may help to protect the eyes from sand when burrowing or when lying half-buried.

In the cool of the night

The sidewinder hunts at night, when it is cooler, rather than during the baking heat of the day. It eats mainly small **mammals** such as mice, plus lizards and the occasional bird. Sidewinders often sit and wait for prey, buried in the sand. Sometimes they follow the scent trail of small mammals or investigate their burrows.

The sidewinder's excellent heat sense is important for helping it to detect prey. In the cool air of the desert night, the warm body of a mammal stands out like a beacon to the sidewinder's **heat sensors**.

Several other snakes have adapted to desert life in a similar way to the sidewinder. The Peringuey's adder has similar colouring, and buries itself in the sand in a similar way.

Classification chart

Scientists classify living things by comparing different kinds and deciding how closely related to each other they are. They then sort them into groups. Different **species** of living things that are closely related are put together in a larger group called a genus (plural genera). Similar genera are grouped into **families**, and similar families are grouped together in orders. Closely related orders are grouped into classes, classes are grouped into phyla and phyla are put together in huge groups called kingdoms. Plants and animals are the two best known kingdoms. Snakes are reptiles (class Reptilia). They are grouped with lizards in the order Squamata. The main snake families are listed below.

The main snake families

Family	Number of species	Examples
Blind snakes (Anomalepididae)	about 20	small thread-like snakes from South America
Thread snakes (Leptotyphlopidae)	80	thread snakes
Blind snakes (Typhlopidae)	over 200	blind snakes
Aniliidae	1	false coral snake
Pipe snakes (Anomochilidae)	2	pipe snakes
Boas and pythons (Boidae)	about 65	anaconda, emerald boa, green tree python, African python, reticulated python
Shield-tailed snakes (Uropeltidae)	about 45	small burrowing snakes from India and Sri Lanka
Atractospididae	about 60	glossy snakes and mole vipers
Colubrids (Colubridae)	over 1500	racer snakes, garter snakes, flying snakes, vine snakes, boomslangs
Elapids (Elapidae)	about 235	cobras, mambas, taipans, coral snakes, kraits, sea snakes
Vipers (Viperidae)	about 150	vipers, adders, rattlesnakes

Where snakes live

These maps show the distribution of different snakes around the world.

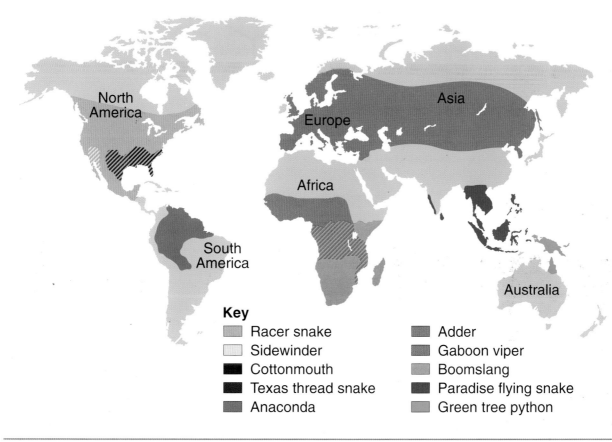

Key

Racer snake		Adder	
Sidewinder		Gaboon viper	
Cottonmouth		Boomslang	
Texas thread snake		Paradise flying snake	
Anaconda		Green tree python	

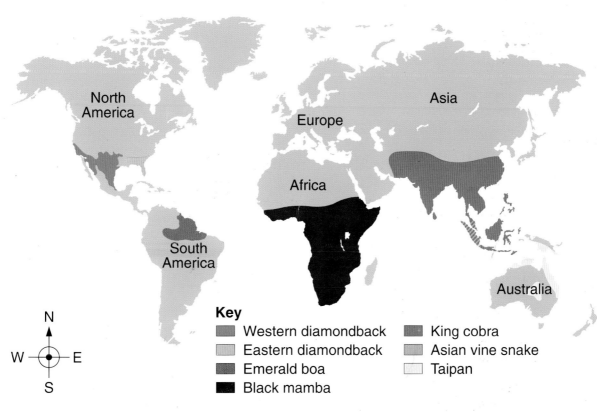

Key

Western diamondback		King cobra	
Eastern diamondback		Asian vine snake	
Emerald boa		Taipan	
Black mamba			

Glossary

acids sour, sharp or corrosive substances. Lemons and vinegar are acid.

adapt/adaptation way in which living things gradually change to fit in with their environment

ancestor relation of a living person or animal that lived many years ago

antibody natural chemical that the body makes to fight off disease or poisons

antivenom medicine that counteracts the poisonous effects of snake venom

caiman type of reptile like an alligator

camouflage colouring and markings on a snake or other animal that help it blend in with its background

cold-blooded animal whose body temperature changes with the temperature of its environment

constrict squeeze

constrictor snake that kills its victims by constricting them rather than by biting

dormant resting

endangered when an animal or plant species is in danger of being wiped out completely

family group or genera of living things that are closely related

fatal deadly

gland organ in the body that produces substances such as tears, saliva (spit) or venom

habitat place where a snake or other creature lives

heat sensor sense organ found in some snakes that can detect heat

hibernate/hibernation going into a deep sleep through the winter

larva (plural larvae) young stage of an insect

ligament thin, strong cord that connects muscles to bones

mammal hairy, warm-blooded animal that feeds its young on breast milk

mangrove tree that grows in swampy conditions along the coasts in some tropical areas

mate/mating when a male inserts sperm into a female animal to fertilize her eggs

oxygen gas found in air and in water that is essential for life

parasite creature that lives on or in another living creature and takes food from it, without giving any benefit in return

peccary pig-like wild animal found in North and South America

pelvis hip bones

predator animal that hunts and eats other animals

prey animal that is hunted by a predator

reproduce to give birth to young or to produce eggs that hatch into young

roost place where birds rest or sleep

savannah grassland with scattered bushes and trees

species group of animals that are very similar and can breed together to produce young

territory area around an animal's den or home that it defends from other animals of the same species

tundra cold, bleak lands that are covered with snow for large parts of the year

venom/venomous poisonous liquid that snakes inject into their prey to kill them. Animals that use venom are said to be venomous.

ventral the underside or front of an animal is its ventral side

warm-blooded animal that can keep its body temperature constant

Further information

Books

Snakes in Question, Carl H. Ernst and George R. Zug (Smithsonian Institution, 1996). The answers to the most frequently asked questions about snakes, written by two of the world's leading experts.

Snakes of the World, Chris Mattison (Cassell Illustrated, 1992). This is a good pocket-sized reference book to the world's snakes, including a description of each snake family.

The Encyclopedia of Snakes, Chris Mattison (Cassell Illustrated, 2002). A bigger, updated and more detailed version of *Snakes of the World*, highly illustrated with excellent photos and pictures.

Classifying Living Things: Reptiles, Andrew Solway (Heinemann Library, 2003). Explores the key features and characteristics of snakes and other reptiles, and how each one is different from the rest.

Websites

www.szgdocent.org/cc/c-main.htm
Excellent website about snakes from the Singapore Zoological Gardens.

www.geocities.com/sceniccityrecords/
Record-breaking reptiles, including the longest, heaviest, oldest and most venomous snakes.

www.qmuseum.qld.gov.au/features/snakes/
A good website on some of the snakes of Australia, including many of the most deadly ones.

www.flyingsnake.org/
A website with videos about flying snakes.

Index